MW00963720

CLIMBING LINCOLN'S STEPS

The African American Journey

by Suzanne Slade   Illustrated by Colin Bootman

Albert Whitman & Company, Chicago, Illinois

Abraham Lincoln was a great leader. When he became president in 1861, many African Americans were enslaved. But Abraham knew slavery must end.

Abraham led America through dark days—when
citizens in the North fought those in the South over slavery
and other issues. Over 600,000 Americans died in the bloody
battles of the Civil War. Abraham had to find a way to end
slavery and unite the country he loved. He spoke out with
brave, honest words. Words that called for freedom for all.

In 1863, Abraham boldly stepped forward for change when he signed the Emancipation Proclamation. This important document freed thousands who were enslaved.

Years passed, but Abraham was not forgotten. In 1914, Americans decided to build a statue in his honor in Washington, D.C. This nineteen-foot masterpiece was created from twenty-eight smaller pieces carved out of white marble—each one carefully chiseled before they were put together like an enormous puzzle. The statue was unveiled to the public in 1922 in a building called the Lincoln Memorial.

Since then, many people have climbed the steps
leading to Abraham's statue—inspired to take another step
for change.

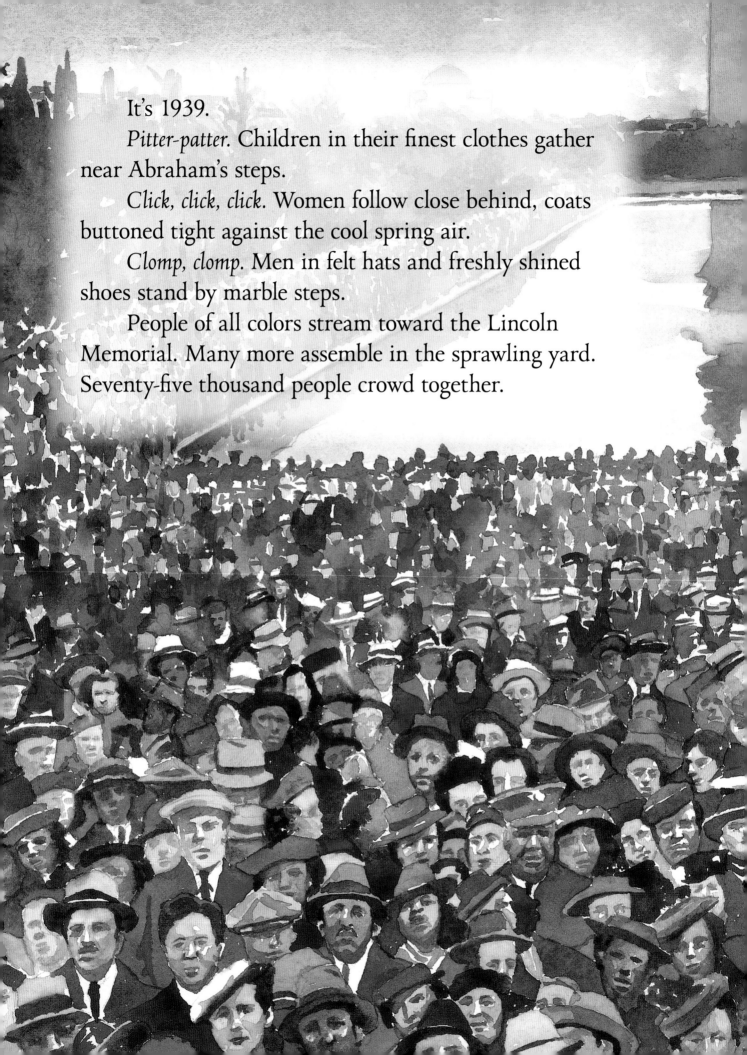

It's 1939.

Pitter-patter. Children in their finest clothes gather near Abraham's steps.

Click, click, click. Women follow close behind, coats buttoned tight against the cool spring air.

Clomp, clomp. Men in felt hats and freshly shined shoes stand by marble steps.

People of all colors stream toward the Lincoln Memorial. Many more assemble in the sprawling yard. Seventy-five thousand people crowd together.

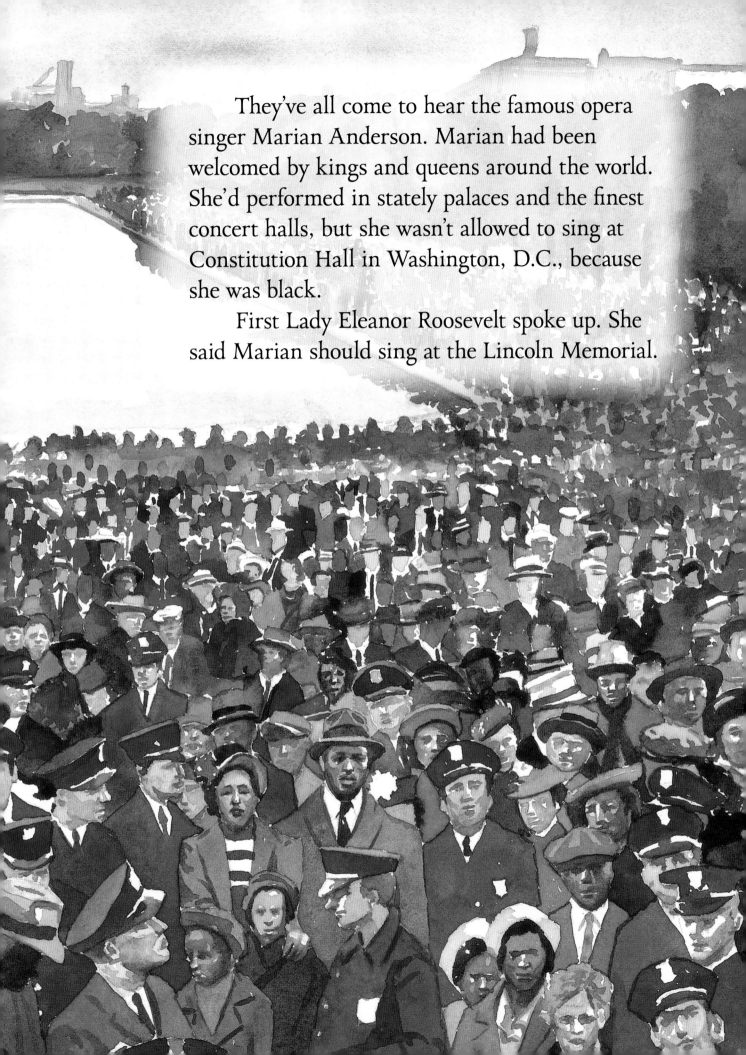

They've all come to hear the famous opera singer Marian Anderson. Marian had been welcomed by kings and queens around the world. She'd performed in stately palaces and the finest concert halls, but she wasn't allowed to sing at Constitution Hall in Washington, D.C., because she was black.

First Lady Eleanor Roosevelt spoke up. She said Marian should sing at the Lincoln Memorial.

That Easter Sunday, Marian's heart pounded wildly as she took her place on top of Abraham's steps. When she began to sing, the thunderous crowd fell silent.

"My country, 'tis of thee, Sweet land of liberty, To thee we sing; Land where my fathers died, Land of our pilgrims' pride . . ."

The sound of change floated through the
fresh April air as Marian sang the song Abraham
had held in his heart.
"From every mountainside, Let freedom ring!"

Microphones carried Marian's magnificent voice over the crowded lawn and into thousands of living room radios across the country. As her voice rose in song, Marian lifted the nation to new heights of understanding—that skill and talent had nothing to do with the color of a person's skin. When the song ended, people cheered. Others wept with joy.

But Americans were still separated—on buses, in
restaurants, and even in schools. Change. It happens slowly.
One
small
step
at a
time.

It's 1963.

People of all colors travel by bus, train, and plane to Washington, D.C. Two hundred thousand march for miles, eager to hear the famous speaker Dr. Martin Luther King, Jr.

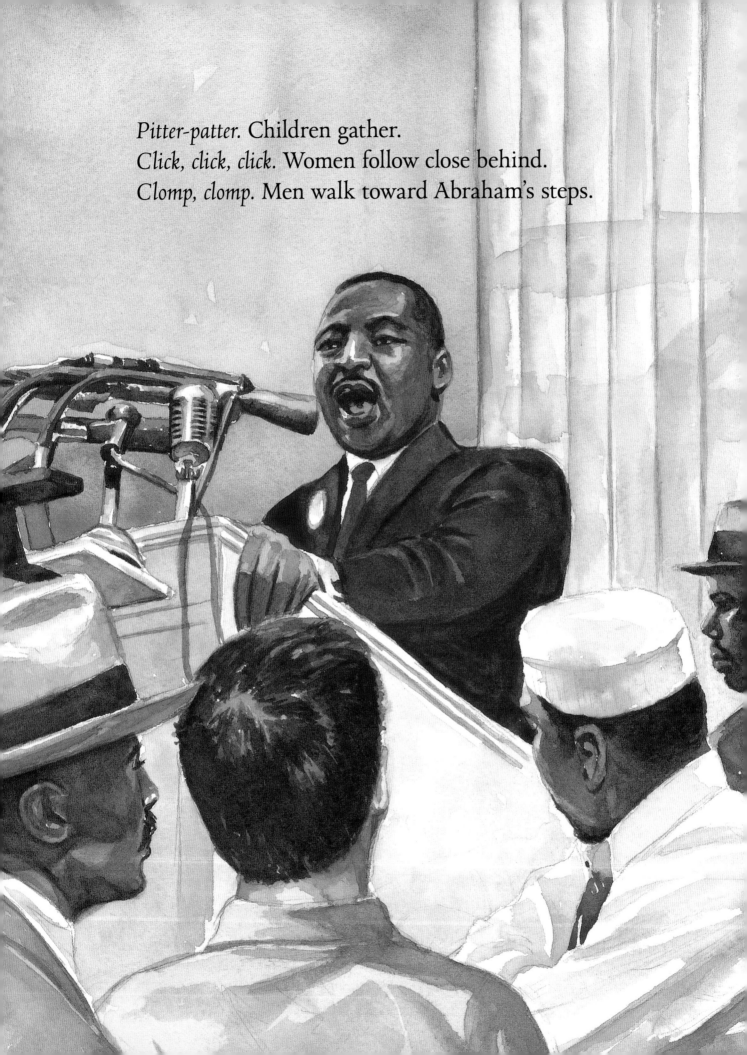

Pitter-patter. Children gather.
Click, click, click. Women follow close behind.
Clomp, clomp. Men walk toward Abraham's steps.

On that hot, sticky August afternoon, Martin shared his dream that one day all Americans would be treated equally. He called for a brighter future where his children would be judged by their character, not by the color of their skin.

Martin's dream echoed across the lawn and crackled over millions of televisions. People listened to the peaceful man with a powerful dream—the same dream Abraham had held in his heart. Martin's speech inspired a nation. Minds opened. Attitudes changed. People united.

Soon, new laws were passed, and it became illegal for hotels, restaurants, and other public places to turn away black people. Everyone was to be given an equal opportunity to buy or rent a house. Businesses could not decide who they hired, or how much they paid workers, based on race.

Although some people didn't like the new laws, more and more Americans realized that everyone deserved equal rights.

Toni
Morrison

Arthur
Ashe

Condoleezza
Rice

Mae
Jemison

Oprah
Winfrey

Change. It happens slowly.

One
small
step
at a
time.

Colin
Powell

Andrew
Young

It's 2009.
Pitter-patter. Two children run up Abraham's steps.
Click, click, click. A woman follows close behind.
Clomp, clomp. One man slowly climbs the famous steps.

The new family that is moving into the big white house a few blocks away—the same house where Abraham once lived—has come to visit.

The girls gaze in awe at the huge statue. Their father studies Abraham's determined face, knowing that although America has come far, there is still more work to be done.

Standing together, the family remembers America's long journey. They remember the people who came before them, those who bravely pressed on and stepped forward for change.

Then Barack Obama, America's first African American president, and his family leave the Lincoln Memorial filled with hope—the same hope Abraham had carried in his heart.

Because change continues to happen.

One

small

step

at a

time.

Steps of Change

Millions of visitors climb Abraham's steps every year to see the statue of the great man who inspired change. Abraham took a major step of change when he signed the Emancipation Proclamation in 1863, but he knew many more would need to step forward to bring true equality and unity to America. Throughout our history, many courageous Americans have taken their own steps for change. Together, these brave people have helped create a better, stronger nation.

Can *you* help make change happen?

Sojourner Truth *took a step when she boldly spoke out for equality for all.*

Many years after being freed from slavery, Isabella Baumfree changed her name to Sojourner Truth. The word "sojourner" means traveler. In 1843 she set out across the country to teach others the truth she lived by—that all people should be treated the same. During her travels, Truth was arrested, threatened, and harassed, but she never stopped teaching. Wherever she spoke, many people gathered. In 1864 Truth met with Abraham Lincoln at the White House. Truth worked for forty years for the rights of black Americans and women.

Frederick Douglass *took a step when he wrote and taught about the evils of slavery.*

Douglass escaped from slavery in 1838 by hiding on a ship bound for New York. A few years later he gave a speech about the horrors of slavery. His speech was so moving that Douglass was invited to speak at other gatherings. In 1845 he published a book about his life as a slave. This powerful narrative convinced many people that slavery was terribly wrong. People who still supported slavery became angry and threatened Douglass. But Douglass did not back down. He continued to write and speak out against enslaving others.

Jackie Robinson *took a step when he showed the world true team spirit.*

When Robinson accepted the Brooklyn Dodgers' invitation to join their team in 1947, he knew it wouldn't be easy to be the first African American baseball player in the major leagues. And he was right—fans threw food at him and called him terrible names. Hotels refused to give him a room, and restaurants wouldn't serve him. But Robinson patiently endured the jeering crowds and humiliation by focusing on the future. He exhibited great self-control, did not respond in anger, and continued to play great ball. Robinson's character and perseverance taught the world that everyone deserves to be treated with respect.

Rosa Parks *took a step when she fought against racial separation.*

On December 1, 1955, Parks made a public stand for civil rights on her way home from work in the segregated city of Montgomery, Alabama. When a bus driver ordered her to give up her seat for a white passenger, Parks politely refused. Although she was arrested and lost her job, her bravery inspired the black citizens of Montgomery to stop riding public buses for a year. This bus boycott ended in December 1956, when the United States Supreme Court said that Alabama's laws separating blacks and whites on buses went against the Constitution. The victory brought national attention to the civil rights cause.

Parks later organized other boycotts and worked with civil rights leaders such as Martin Luther King. Her courageous actions led many Americans to see that racial separation was wrong.

TIMELINE

1838   Frederick Douglass escapes from slavery. He becomes an author, speaker, and civil rights leader.

1863   Abraham Lincoln signs the Emancipation Proclamation.

1864   Sojourner Truth meets with President Lincoln at the White House.

1922   The Lincoln Memorial is completed. Henry Bacon designed the grand building. Sculptor Daniel Chester French carved Lincoln's statue with the help of six carvers from the Piccirilli family.

1939   Marian Anderson sings at the Lincoln Memorial. That historic day, Marian sang "to thee we sing" instead of the usual lyrics "of thee I sing." She also changed the words "the pilgrims' pride" to "our pilgrims' pride," perhaps sending a message that liberty and freedom belong to all Americans.

1947   Jackie Robinson joins the Brooklyn Dodgers and becomes the first African American player in National League baseball.

1955   Rosa Parks makes a stand for civil rights, refusing to give up her seat on the bus to a white person.

1963   Martin Luther King gives his "I Have A Dream" speech at the Lincoln Memorial.

1975   Arthur Ashe wins the men's singles title at the Wimbledon tennis championships in England. That same year, he is ranked as the number one male tennis player in the world.

1977   Andrew Young is appointed the first African American U.S. ambassador to the United Nations.

1983   Oprah Winfrey becomes the first female African American television host.

1992   Mae Jemison blasts off as the first female African American astronaut.

1993   Toni Morrison is the first African American awarded the Nobel Prize in Literature.

2001   Colin Powell becomes the first African American U.S. secretary of state.

2005   Condoleezza Rice is named the first female African American U.S. secretary of state.

2009   Barack Obama is sworn in as the first African American president of the United States.

To Sally Hunsberger, who strives for change that brings peace;
Sharon Stevens, who guides teens toward positive change;
and Mary Allen, who inspires change for a better America.—S.S.

To the spirit of change and the belief that we who know struggle will, ultimately, see better days.—C.B.

Library of Congress Cataloging-in-Publication Data

Slade, Suzanne.
Climbing Lincoln's steps : the African American journey / Suzanne Slade ; illustrated by Colin Bootman.
p. cm.
ISBN 978-0-8075-1204-3
1. United States—Race relations—History—Juvenile literature. 2. African Americans—Civil rights—History—Juvenile literature.
3. Lincoln Memorial (Washington, D.C.)—History—Juvenile literature.
4. Lincoln, Abraham, 1809-1865—Monuments—Washington (D.C.)—Juvenile literature. I. Bootman, Colin. II. Title.
E185.61.S618 2010   305.800973—dc22   2010004962

Text copyright © 2010 by Suzanne Slade. Illustrations copyright © 2010 by Colin Bootman.
Published in 2010 by Albert Whitman & Company.
All rights reserved. No part of this book may be reproduced or transmitted in any form or by any means, electronic or mechanical,
including photocopying, recording, or by any information storage and retrieval system, without permission in writing from the publisher.
Printed in China.
10 9 8 7 6 5 4 BP 15 14 13 12

The art is rendered in watercolor on paper.
The design is by Carol Gildar.

For more information about Albert Whitman & Company, please visit our web site at www.albertwhitman.com.